HOW DOES IT WORK?
MOTORCYCLES

by Joanne Mattern

pogo

Ideas for Parents and Teachers

Pogo Books let children practice reading informational text while introducing them to nonfiction features such as headings, labels, sidebars, maps, and diagrams, as well as a table of contents, glossary, and index.

Carefully leveled text with a strong photo match offers early fluent readers the support they need to succeed.

Before Reading

- "Walk" through the book and point out the various nonfiction features. Ask the student what purpose each feature serves.
- Look at the glossary together. Read and discuss the words.

Read the Book

- Have the child read the book independently.
- Invite him or her to list questions that arise from reading.

After Reading

- Discuss the child's questions. Talk about how he or she might find answers to those questions.
- Prompt the child to think more. Ask: What did you know about motorcycles before you read this book? What more do you want to learn after reading it?

Pogo Books are published by Jump!
5357 Penn Avenue South
Minneapolis, MN 55419
www.jumplibrary.com

Copyright © 2018 Jump!
International copyright reserved in all countries.
No part of this book may be reproduced in any form without written permission from the publisher.

Library of Congress Cataloging-in-Publication Data

Names: Mattern, Joanne, 1963- author.
Title: Motorcycles / by Joanne Mattern.
Description: Minneapolis, MN : Jump!, Inc., [2018]
Series: How does it work? | Audience: Ages 7-10.
Identifiers: LCCN 2017029895 (print) | LCCN 2017030257 (ebook) | ISBN 9781624966989 (ebook)
ISBN 9781620319086 (hardcover : alk. paper)
ISBN 9781620319093 (pbk.)
Subjects: LCSH: Motorcycles–Juvenile literature.
Classification: LCC TL440.15 (ebook)
LCC TL440.15 .M38 2017 (print) | DDC 629.227/5–dc23
LC record available at https://lccn.loc.gov/2017029895

Editor: Jenna Trnka
Book Designer: Leah Sanders
Photo Researcher: Leah Sanders

Photo Credits: Great Art Productions/Getty, cover; droopy76/Shutterstock, 1; wikanda/Shutterstock, 3; SeanShot/iStock, 4; bondvit/Shutterstock, 5; Aliaksandr Zosimau/Shutterstock, 6-7; imamember/iStock, 8-9; frank'n'focus/Alamy, 10; Lukas Gojda/Shutterstock, 11; Africa Studio/Shutterstock, 12-13; MorePixels/Getty, 14; Ivan Garcia/Shutterstock, 15; taelove7/Shutterstock, 16-17; James Steidl/Shutterstock, 18-19; stockphoto mania/Shutterstock, 20-21; MarcelClemens/Shutterstock, 23.

Printed in the United States of America at Corporate Graphics in North Mankato, Minnesota.

TABLE OF CONTENTS

CHAPTER 1

PARTS OF A MOTORCYCLE

Have you ever seen a motorcycle? Maybe you've ridden on one! A motorcycle moves on two wheels, just like a bicycle. But a motorcycle is much more powerful. And fast!

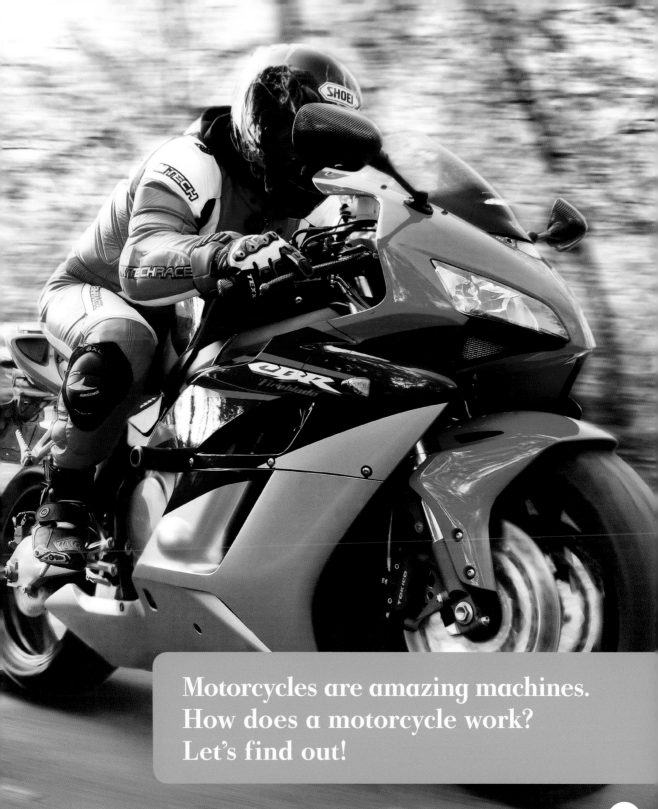

Motorcycles are amazing machines.
How does a motorcycle work?
Let's find out!

Many parts make a motorcycle go. What makes a motorcycle powerful is its **engine**. Gas goes into the gas tank. Gas fuels the engine. It makes the motorcycle go.

DID YOU KNOW?

Some early bike engines were powered with **steam**. In 1885, a gas-powered engine was added to a bike. This was the first motorcycle.

gas tank

engine

muffler

A motorcycle engine produces waste gases. These gases flow out of an exhaust pipe. The exhaust pipe is on the back of the bike. Exhaust pipes also have **mufflers**. Mufflers make motorcycles quieter.

CHAPTER 2

HOW IT WORKS

How does a motorcycle work? Gas flows into the engine. It mixes with air. A **spark plug** burns the gas. This **energy** turns **gears** inside the engine. These gears send power to the wheels.

The wheels turn and move the motorcycle. The driver steers by using handlebars. Turning the handlebars turns the front wheel.

To stop a motorcycle, the driver squeezes a lever on the handlebar. That lever moves clips on the tires. The clips squeeze the tire. This creates **friction**. It makes the tire stop. This slows and stops the bike.

TAKE A LOOK!

All the parts of a motorcycle work together. Energy moves from the gas tank to the engine. The engine sends that energy to the back wheel. The wheel moves the motorcycle. Handlebars steer the front wheel.

■ = handlebars
■ = exhaust pipe
■ = engine

■ = gas tank
■ = muffler
■ = wheels

CHAPTER 3

MANY KINDS OF MOTORCYCLES

There are many kinds of motorcycles. Touring motorcycles are big. They have large gas tanks and strong engines. They are made for long road trips.

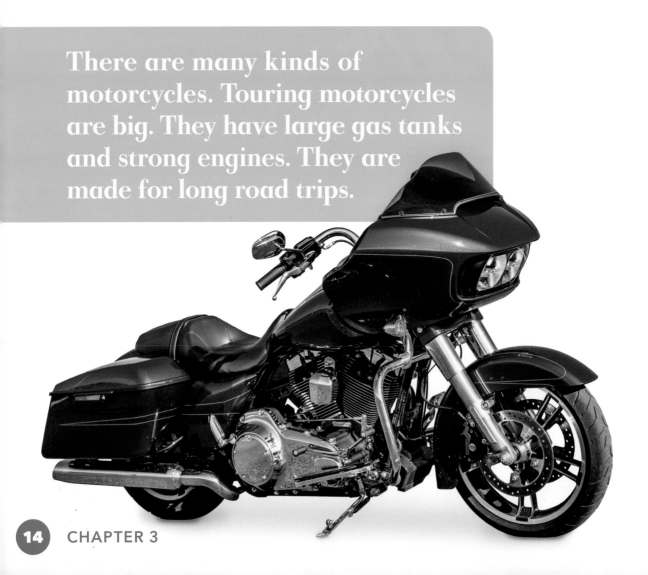

Sport bikes **accelerate** quickly. They are fast. Drivers race them on tracks. They can make sharp corners.

Dirt bikes are small motorcycles. Some people race dirt bikes. They race them on trails or dirt roads. These bikes have light **frames**. They are easier to control. They make jumps. Their tires have deep **tread**. These tires are great for gripping dirt or mud.

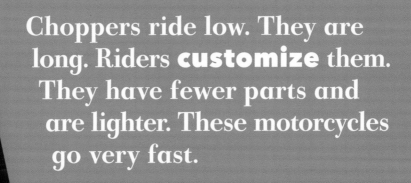

Choppers ride low. They are long. Riders **customize** them. They have fewer parts and are lighter. These motorcycles go very fast.

DID YOU KNOW?

The fastest motorcycle in the world can reach a top speed of 350 miles (563 kilometers) per hour. That is almost five times faster than everyday cars drive!

Motorcycles are fun to ride but can be dangerous. Drivers are experienced. They learn how to handle their bike. They wear protective clothing and helmets.

Motorcycles are fast and loud! Which kind of bike is your favorite?

ACTIVITIES & TOOLS

HOW DO WHEELS WORK?

Wheels are important parts of motorcycles. Axles are the rods in the centers of wheels that wheels revolve around. See how they work!

What You Need:
- two plastic straws
- packing tape
- scissors
- cardboard
- hole punch

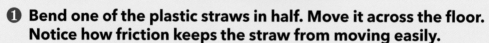

❶ Bend one of the plastic straws in half. Move it across the floor. Notice how friction keeps the straw from moving easily.

❷ Cut four small circles out of cardboard.

❸ Use the hole punch to make a hole in the middle of each cardboard circle.

❹ Cut two small pieces from the second straw.

❺ Push one piece of straw through two of the circles to make an axle and wheels.

❻ Repeat step #5 with the second piece of straw and the other two cardboard circles to make a second set of wheels.

❼ Use packing tape to attach the two sets of wheels and axles to each end of the first straw to make a bike.

❽ Move the bike across the floor. It is easier to move because the wheels turn and cut down on friction.

GLOSSARY

accelerate: To gain speed.

customize: To build, rebuild, or alter something to the way you want it.

energy: Power that is used to operate a machine.

engine: A machine that changes energy into movement.

frames: The basic structures on which motorcycles are built.

friction: The resistance created when one surface rubs against another.

gears: Sets of wheels with teeth that fit together and perform a function in a machine.

mufflers: Devices that reduce the noise made by an engine.

spark plug: The part of a gas engine that creates a spark to ignite the fuel.

steam: Vapor formed when water boils.

tread: The part of a wheel that makes contact with the ground.

INDEX

TO LEARN MORE

Learning more is as easy as 1, 2, 3.

1) Go to www.factsurfer.com

2) Enter "motorcycles" into the search box.

3) Click the "Surf" button to see a list of websites.

With factsurfer, finding more information is just a click away.